*Simple Words
for a more
Elegant Time*

Simple Words for a more Elegant Time

ANDREW GREENHALGH

THE CHOIR PRESS

First published in the United Kingdom in 2021 by
The Choir Press

ISBN 978-1-78963-186-9

Louise,
You opened the door, but I had to walk through it.

My Parents,
Always there with a helping hand.

Contents

Opening Words

Number 1

The anticipation in the air was electric. The crowd stood as the first rays tentatively emerged over the horizon. A silence slowly swept through the gathering, as each reflected upon all that had taken place and to mourn the loss of those who had not made it this far. Their journey had been slow and difficult, their accomplishments many and varied.

The glow of light crept across the scene before them with increasing speed. Who could say what was in front of them? Whilst history is stoic and unalterable, the future is forgiving and full of possibilities.

Reflections and Dreams

Number 2

This is a tall tale told by a fool and an idiot, words of indecision and jest bringing chaos and derision.

Magical moments cast into doubt by fractured light, and displaced sound.

A city on a hill surrounded, encompassed, pressed with earnestness and vigour, held low by the words of a few.

Number 3

I see you in the corner of my mind through the floating shadows of the sun's golden rays, an interstitial wrap of time and space, folded in upon uncertainty, creating confusion and worry.

Words are powerful things: a record of the past, and a doorway to the future.

Step forward, run, smile or laugh. A single stone thrown into life's pond touches many shores.

Number 4

Let us journey on this difficult track, this pathway to infinity.

Let us behold all that we can be, and struggle to find our way.

Let us see when we are blinded to all that is beautiful around us.

Let us speak of things when we are choked, and too scared to say a word.

Let us begin; tomorrow is too late.

Number 5

The tree watched the moon rise on this cold night. After this all would be different.

Throughout time the tree had seen it all: love, hate, fear, poverty, war and suffering. But this night was the last night of darkness.

Times change, people grow old and die, and ideas flourish and fade.

The tree knew eventually everything turns to ash, but for those with butterfly life-spans a moment of joy can last forever.

The witching hour had arrived, when all time stops, and now it has past all life begins, a new day is born. Finally, a new day, a new era, and peace at last.

Number 6

As I look back on all that I have been, and all that I was, I have to ask, did I dream, or was it real?

For I have walked with giants and laughed with elves, seen music in the rain and songs in the sun; my illusions of light and time transfixed all but the muse in my mind.

Who are we but travellers in our own time, living in the endless sea of night, not caring or believing in anything but our own light?

For all that I was has been like a heartbeat in the shadows of a forgotten dream, and all that I can be will be a light for tomorrow's hopes.

A muse for one, guide for many and belief for all.

Number 7

Let us begin our journey. One foot follows the last.

We walk through mists and fire, happiness and sorrow, fear and pain.

I feel your music through the rain and see it dance across the glistening ice of a winter's morning. Each note resonates against my mind, flooding my soul with haunting melodies.

I see all that can be, my hopes and dreams, simple steps forward.

Guide me through, or push me fast: my journey must be finished.

Number 8

I see the world stretch out in front of me. Rolling fields of straw, cut short, stacked neat for all to see. Autumn's animals running and foraging, preparing their beds for the long snuggle against the night.

Golden swifts dance and weave on bands of sunlight, as rabbits hop and slide on soft dew-covered grass.

Gentle winds rustle leaves, and pluck them from their branches.

I see the world change, green to red, then to brown. I gather my home above and around me, preparing for the dark. Spines stretched out, all curled up, ready for my sleep.

Number 9

I sit and watch her walk; she moves and flows, yet stumbles and staggers.

Her footfalls fail as she folds herself low. I move to stand, but stop and watch. She reads and whispers, voice so faint.

She stands again, papers held low, trailing behind her, yet caught in her wake. Words falling, drifting to the floor, to rest upon the shadow of her steps. My heart stops as she passes me by, face taut and sad.

Curiosity flows through me as my eyes drift to the words crumpled so low, each page follows the first and flows to the last, to an end so sudden and sad. I straighten the first so it meets the last and notice her purpose.

"My past is past, my future is without you."

She looks back and smiles, now not so blue.

Number 10

I see the mist behind your mask, your eyes lost in time and distant spaces.

Who are you?
I do not know.
What have you seen?
I do not know.

We all carry masks, but for some their mask is a shield to keep the darkness away.

Number 11

The notes from your fingers drum gently against their minds. Haunting strings dance under taut fingers to a chorus of ivory smiles, touching distant memories.

This simplification of music and beat tiptoes across the strings of time.

Moments fall like petals from yesterday's rose, and past dreams flicker against life's mirror.

Where do you stand? Are you a reflection, or the dream?

Number 12

The warriors faced each other, all courtesies extended, all promises met. Silhouetted against the night by the gently falling snow. Their blades shimmered as the moonlight danced along the steel. The pause stretched out as each warrior sank deeper into the moment, waiting for the first mistake, their battle fought between the empty space of slowed breathing and flashing neurons. Each move and counter move, blocked, defeated and overcome. Preparation, study and focus.

A glisten of steel, a rustle of fabric and then a blurring of movement. Only one stands.

"Ready?"

"Yes I am. You see it is all about visualising. I have prepared, I have studied and I am focused."

"Well then. Your piece is J.S. Bach Concerto in A minor. Let the exam begin."

Messages from the Heart

Number 13

You are my muse, my guide, my silver lining to my darkest cloud.

You are my morning sun, which illuminates my darkened path.

You are the spirt of my purpose, my wish upon a falling star.

You are my warmth against the coldest night and my sweetest love, forever and a day.

Number 14

I close my eyes, I see you in my dreams.
I hear the warmth of your voice.
I feel the softness of your touch.
I open my heart, I surrender my senses.

I kiss your lips with the softest embrace.
I feel your body melt into my arms.
I see time slow as we continue to kiss.

Each moment of my life is but a shard of time, to be held, to be felt, to be lived.

For me time has stopped since the moment we first kissed.

Number 15

A beginning is a difficult place, a time-filled moment empty
but yet full, passing from one point to the next.

We see the spaces in time as lost hours, confined to the cellars
of our lives, forgotten like lost dreams from the night.

The beauty of a perfect moment flows and drifts, like a
fleeting kiss.

Time is a lover, embraced by all, but loved by few.

Number 16

She opened her eyes to the ever-increasing glow of the morning light, and the gentle sound of padding feet.

'Going?' she murmured from beneath the folds of crisp white sheets, dappled by the morning sunlight.

'Just for a moment,' he replied as he crossed to the bed to kneel at her side, lightly kissing the skin of her bare shoulder.

'Cold!' she giggled as she moved closer to him and felt the feather-like touch of the embrace against her lips, and the electric feel of goose bumps from his hand slowly caressing her skin, extending the moment to a timeless infinity.

'Still going?' she asked as she pulled him closer, feeling the warmth of his body against her.

'Never,' he replied as he stepped off the grains of rice on the bedroom floor.

Number 17

I stand and wait. I look and watch. The words behind the notes, the pages behind the music, guide us when we cannot see. The infinite beat of time taps against life's melody.

I have been and always shall be with you, my friend, my love, my angel with a mischievous smile.

To part is a deep sadness, a sorrow quenched only by time and distance.

Number 18

You are my muse, my angel and my inspiration.

Each evening I think of you before I sleep, holding you, loving you.

Each morning I wake and my first thoughts are of you.

To be in love is wonderful; to have met one's true love is bliss.

Words from
the Night

Number 19

The flame flickers in a breeze, dancing and twisting. It illuminates the night providing a point of light, a focus for all around.

We see ourselves as a reflection in others, our moods, our fears, and our goals. We are driven or pushed by our futures' end; unconsciously moving to create that which we hold dear, however, at times we inexplicably bend to the will of those around us.

We feel the energy of the flame within us, its strength. We feel that which we should be and that which we are. For we are all things; but we choose not to believe them.

Number 20

A flickering candle stands alone; its light barely glows against the jet-black night. To some it is alone in the dark without companionship or awareness. To others it is a guide, a beacon to navigate the dark.

We all carry candles within us, to guide the hearts of others out of the darkness.

Number 21

A word is a powerful thing, it can bring two people together, or push them apart; it can form new alliances, and create new friends. All words have an opposite side, which detracts from their true intention: one side black, and one side white.

To describe you is to become lost in love, passion, and fire. To touch you is to feel the warmest of embraces, the softest of kisses. To be with you is to feel a pause in time, a moment stretched out to infinity.

A word is a powerful thing. For you there can be only true words. Words from the heart are never forgotten.

Number 22

We see through open eyes, but we do not see all that is around us; we can look for hours, and not see the wood for the trees.

Who we are and what we are is generally based on what others think of us, not what we think of ourselves. We are all special. We simply just need to look.

Number 23

I am illusion.
I am mist.
I am ether.

What am I?
A dream, a memory of faded times, an image on a dusty photograph.

Who am I?
Am I real or virtual, embodied or separate?

Perception is who we are, a mouse can roar like a lion to someone who has never seen either before.

All of these things are what we see, or believe we see. All things change to the path they were supposed to follow.

In the end.
We are what we are.
We are who we are.
We love whom we are supposed to love.

Number 24

What is music but a collection of notes?
What is a note but a collection of letters?
What is a letter but a collection of thoughts?
What is a thought but a collection of insights?

All these things lead on from one another.
All these things are bound to one another.
All these things are apart, without one another.

We are bound together for all time, apart in body, but
together in spirit.

Number 25

A butterfly gracefully dances from leaf to flower, kissing each one as it moves. It knows its place and all around it. The breeze comes from nowhere and steals the butterfly away, carrying it to new and distant place. All is strange, but the same.

A butterfly gracefully dances from leaf to flower, kissing each one as it moves. It knows its place and all around it. The breeze comes from nowhere and steals the butterfly away, carrying it to new and distant place. All is strange, but the same.

What is familiar, and what is strange; the world is full of change. Here comes a strong wind.

Number 26

Dust falls from the faded image of life's mirror, of long distant memories of hopes and dreams, yesterday's promises and ambitions, lost chances and goals.

Age brings forth all worries and concerns, and future hopes drift in on an uncertain sea.

We all see the past through rose-coloured glass, ignoring the darkness and pain as we drink back to more joyous times of peace and wellbeing.

We all see the things that made us, like drifting sands caught up in the winds of fate.

What is change? Simply that which has not been. Change is the future!

Number 27

Who are we but grains of sand cast into the sky on a moonless night, tiny and obscure in our insignificance, our purpose unknown?

We look into the blackness of the depthless night and see our hopes and dreams rise and glow.

We are chargers, strong and agile, focused and determined. We are the night and the day; they are part of us, a balance, and a counter. We know that for all things there are two sides, two ways to see.

We only see what we wish to see, but we feel all things. That is our problem, which is our folly.

Number 28

Everything we see is from the past, light and sound.
All of the images we take for granted are old; nothing is
current.

No one is in fashion, because everything is retro.
Who are we, but faded images from a distant past?
Are you the woman I saw before, or just a ghost of times long
past?

Number 29

I stand to the south, the sun on my face, warming me, comforting me.

I turn and look to the distant horizon. I see them coming closer, dust trailing from their path, their vehicles bumping along, rolling through the dunes.

They come closer. I see the joy and happiness in their faces as they speed by, leaving a swirl of sand and dust around me.

Their journey, their adventures are still to come. But they will walk in the fading footprints of those who have gone before them; and we shall be their guides. That is our promise.

Number 30

I stand before the door: the gateway to tomorrow, a portal to the past.

Who have I become?
Where is my past?
Who will be my future?

I have stood at the beginning of time and seen all that will be, created from all that was. I have stood at the end of days and seen all that was drift by like sand in the wind.

I am the shield, the darkness against the light, forever in shadows awaiting my day. But what is dark, and what is light; to one another they are alike?

Time is the key to all things; it forms the basis of all life and death, the beginning to the end.

Time is the key to the essence of life, our hopes and dreams.

Is life the illusion, or is the dream the reality?

Number 31

I am a million years old.

I have moved through time from all that was ancient, to all that is current.

I have seen the brightest star and the darkness night.

In each of those moments, I have seen only reflections of myself in the faces of those with fleeting lifespans, as they drift by.

The fullness of time is wasted on those without purpose or goals. Infinity creates only monotony and tedium.

Number 32

We all look back through life's long mirror and dance between the rain drops of memories past.

Reflections without substance yield only vanity without life.

If we move forward without certainty, look without purpose, we miss those who stride forward with small steps.

Winter and Snow

Number 33

Let me take you by the hand and show you my world of music and light, of dancing elves and reindeer flying through the night.

Christmas comes but once a year, the lights, the sounds, and the sense of delight.

A world apart, a world together, peace and joy, for all and forever.

Number 34

Winter's gaze lingers and settles in, as tendrils of frozen fingers creep across the ground, chasing birds to warmer climes and driving animals to scurry and hide. All is warm behind a ball of pointed spikes.

Gentle laughter rolled around the room, glasses clinking against each other to toast peace and joy.

Silence throughout the smaller rooms as excitement keeps tired eyes open, before reluctant sleep takes hold.

Snuggled whiskers and fur rest against warm bodies wrapped in soft coverings and blankets.

Peace and calm settles against the night as a solitary figure glides and flows between walls and chimneys, doors and gates. With a smile and a wink, a ho and a ho, a figure in red slowly disappears into the night.

"Mum, can we go now?"

"Yes, off you go, and don't forget to bring back some sweet mincemeat pies, they are very nice."

Two small, white, furry blurs jump from floor to chair, then to table.

"The Red One is very messy." "Yes, but it does leave behind nice food," said the mouse to her sister.

Number 35

Lights fade as the clinking of glasses grows distant and night's darkness starts to recede.

Choruses of wellbeing and joy drift on early morning air, as houses calm and doors close.

The first shards of light cast their glow as pathways through misty air, illuminating long furry ears as eyes dart quickly and long legs hop through the light.

One path illuminates the next, then another as the light spreads, always moving, always changing. The integrated flow of time and space, decision and thought, constantly moving forward revealing our path.

For we have always been time travellers within our own time. One step forward across the threshold, no looking back, a new dawn, a new day, a new year.

Number 36

I cannot remember how long I have been falling. Tumbling, and twisting through the sky.

I look around me, to see if the others are following my lead, hoping I am not alone in the swirl.

I look down: my view is obscured. I panic. I cannot see my friends. Am I lost, or off course?

The wind has brought me through the trees. I see the ground coming up fast, causing me to roll and flail, and then I am safe, snuggled up against the other snowflakes.

Number 37

There it was again, the soft tinkling of laughter drifting across the valley, stronger now as they made their yearly walk through the winter snows, so deep this year.

Their walk was always hard, but with their young it had proved to be so treacherous on the slopes and hills. Each step had become an effort, and a worry that had started to run through the group. Why, why had they started this? There was no need, but for a silly tradition, the words on the lips of the elders, as they looked at their young falling through the snow.

Too late to stop, too late to return, now too late to slow down. Why, why?

"I see a glow," shouted one. "No, it is a light!" shouted another. Finally! A sigh flowed through the group.

Finally they could rest. They all sat down, and waited in the clearing.

For those still awake it would have seemed strange to see one, even two, but there in the dark and cold of the night was a line of white polar bears, sitting quietly to watch a man in bright red fur flying on a sled between the village huts, as stealthy as any bear, dropping sacks at every door.

As quick as they blinked the man flew high and fast over them and then dove down to their line. Not a word was said, not a movement made. For this was their test, their trial. "Maybe next year?" They heard as the man flew away. Red parcels left before them. Ho, ho, ho.

Number 38

We begin our journey through the eerie calm of the dark night, floating on gossamer wings, dancing and skating to the beat of unheard music.

We fall like petals from an autumn blown flower.

Our lives are cool, fleeting and unique, brief pauses from the intensity of time, individual moments lost to history.

I land. I squeeze and nestle up to my friends.

'Ah Mum, it's snowing!' giggled the little girl as she looked out of the window.

Number 39

A winter's night descends across the town. Cut ribbons and threaded bows, sweet mince pies, and fresh iced cakes.

Dusty boxes descend from lofty spaces, packed so tight, memories jumbled on top of each other. Items brought forth and hung, twisted and turned until they fit so perfectly. A model event, a perfect show, recorded and snapped in an instant for all to see.

Distant moments of joy sound across the house, thundering over floors and rattling walls.

Pressed and smoothed linen, gleaming white plates, and crystal flowing with bubbles adorn the tables. Smiles and laughter with toasts held high.

A special day, a Christmas Day, a magical moment for all.

Number 40

The snow burns my eyes; I feel it swirl about my feet.
I try to struggle on but I cannot move forward.
I hear the hordes call to me, cry to me.
I try to move. I drag my tired legs.
I cannot move. I am trapped in ice, held fast.
I hear the pack coming for me, trampling over friend and foe.
I feel frozen in place, set and held fast.
I hear them, closer now; the earth shakes from their rampage.
I bend my will to move my feet, now a stump of coldness and ice.
I see them now, all is lost.
I am done for: my escape is now impossible.

"There he is!" Cry the children as they throw their snowballs at the snowman.

Number 41

The lights sparkle against the firmament of the night.

Glitter drifts down from the ceiling as the last cork falls. Happy sleepy smiles fade, and go distant as the final door closes. Peace, calm and reflection.

The world sighs and breathes anew, the moments between moments when all is still.

Progress is forward from reflection and resolution.

"Ready for the New Year?"

A Few More Words

Number 42

For the final time I cast myself into the void, to stride and roll in lyrical excellence, to dance upon a word, and drift upon a phrase.

What brings us to this place but a collection of thoughts of times long past? What takes us to the next place: a plane, a boat, a truck bouncing down a dusty road?

A tree falls in a forest, and there is no one to hear it fall, does it make a noise? Who cares! Important events should be seen, and their effects felt.

So to the end, for truly there is no end, for all that we have been resides in the things we have done, and the words we have written. The future is but a blur of unfocused choices, and actions waiting to be experienced.

Lightning Source UK Ltd.
Milton Keynes UK
UKHW010643070421
381585UK00001B/121